My CHRISTMAS

Activity Book

Catherine Mackenzie
Puzzles and Illustrations
by Kim Shaw

CF4•K

DEDICATION:

For Molly Padfield –
our little Christmas card friend.
May you come to love Jesus
even more than Christmas!
Catherine

For my four wonderful grandchildren,
Zoe, Jack, Benjamin and Rebecca.
Kim

What's in this Book?

10 9 8 7 6 5 4 3 2
Copyright © 2016 Christian Focus Publications
ISBN: 978-1-78191-759-6
Reprinted in 2017
Published by
Christian Focus Publications,
Geanies House, Fearn, Tain, Ross-shire, IV20 1TW, U.K.
Text by Catherine Mackenzie
Cover design by Daniel van Straaten
Illustrations by Kim Shaw
Printed and bound by Bell and Bain

FSC
www.fsc.org
MIX
Paper from
responsible sources
FSC® C007785

Some Bible quotations are the author's own paraphrase but unless otherwise stated all other Scripture quotations are from The Holy Bible, English Standard Version, copyright © 2001 by Crossway Bibles, a division of Good News Publishers. Used by permission. All rights reserved. ESV Text Edition: 2007. Scripture taken from the HOLY BIBLE, NEW INTERNATIONAL VERSION®. NIV®. Copyright©1973, 1978, 1984 by International Bible Society. Used by permission of Zondervan. All rights reserved.

Jesus' Birth

For to us a child is born, to us a son is given; and the government shall be upon his shoulder, and his name shall be called Wonderful Counsellor, Mighty God, Everlasting Father, Prince of Peace.

Isaiah 9:6

1. The First Christmas Promise

When God made the world, it was perfect. It was very good. Picture in your mind the beautiful hills and skies without any pollution. Imagine all the amazing animals and birds – none of them extinct. Now think about how different our world is today. It has been spoilt. How did this happen? The first people that God created, Adam and Eve, were told not to eat from one particular tree – The Tree of Knowledge of Good and Evil. If they did, they would die. They would disobey God. That is what we call sinning. Everything was perfect until the evil one, the devil, appeared as a serpent and deceived Eve into eating from that tree. Adam ate it too. They tried to hide their sin from God, but hiding anything from God is impossible. God told Adam and Eve that they had to be punished. Their lives would be exhausting and painful, and eventually they would die. But God gave them a promise too – a promise of hope. One day a Saviour would come, who would defeat sin. Many years later, God sent his Son to this world. He was born in a small town called Bethlehem. His name was Jesus.

Look It Up:
Genesis 3:14-15

Colour it in and Work it Out

Unjumble the letters to find out what colour each bit of the picture should be: lenag (yellow) lothsec (brown) eter (brown/green) wsodr (silver) arih (black) asnke (red/yellow)

2. Abraham's Promise

Many years passed, but God did not forget his promise. He had a plan to rescue sinners. Who is a sinner? Well, everyone is. Even the newest baby, born on this very day, does not love or obey God perfectly. Human beings are born wanting to disobey God. Without God's love, sinners would stay sinners forever. And all sin must be punished. However, God's plan was to save sinners by giving their punishment to someone else. God would send his Son to this world as a human baby. God's Son would be called Jesus, and it would be Jesus who would take the punishment for sin.

God had to keep reminding people throughout history that the Saviour was on his way. He did this with a man called Abraham. Abraham and his wife, Sarah, had no children. But God promised them a son. He also promised Abraham that, through him, all the families in the world would be happy and blessed. When they were very old, the promised son arrived, and they named him Isaac. This baby reminded them that God was faithful and that one day he would send the Saviour.

This really happened. Look at Abraham's family tree – there's one special person in it – the Lord Jesus Christ.

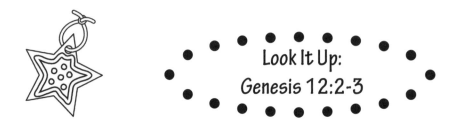

Look It Up:
Genesis 12:2-3

Bible Art!

Here we have Abraham, Sarah and their precious baby son.
Something for you to colour in.

3. Micah's Promise

Throughout history, God continued to remind his people about his promise. It was such an amazing promise – it's strange to think that people would forget about it… but they did. They often forgot about what God had told them. Sometimes they even chose to ignore it.

God chose special people called prophets to go and speak to the people. These men would remind them of the things that God had said. They would warn the people about sin and tell them that it displeased God. And then they would try to encourage the people by telling them again and again that God loved them, and that he wanted to forgive them. Several times God would give the prophets a special message called a prophecy. The prophets would hear God telling them about something that would happen in the future. One of the prophets, Micah, was told that the promised Saviour would be born in a little town called Bethlehem. 'But you, O Bethlehem Ephrathah, who are too little to be among the clans of Judah, from you shall come forth for me one who is to be ruler in Israel, whose coming forth is from of old, from ancient days.' (Micah 5:2) These messages and prophecies were written down so that the people could read them for themselves.

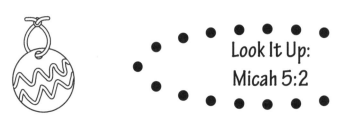

Look It Up:
Micah 5:2

Crack the Code

Can you decipher Micah's message?

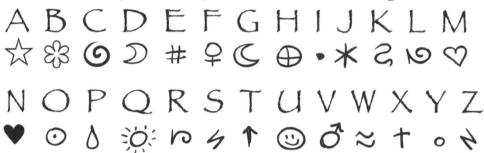

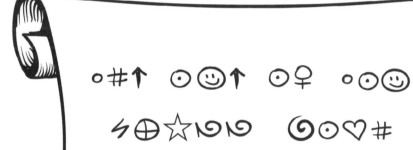

(NKJV) The answers for the codes and wordsearches
are at the back of the book.

4. Isaiah's Promise

The prophet Isaiah also received a special message from God. This prophecy was about how the promised Saviour would be born – just like you and me, but that one thing would be very different.

The promised Saviour would be born to a virgin. What does this mean? Well, it meant that the mother of the promised Saviour would not have a husband. Mary, the young girl who became the mother of the promised Saviour, Jesus, had never been married. She had never done anything that would have made a baby inside her – but God performed a miracle. His power overshadowed her, and the Son of God became a little bunch of cells, a human life inside the womb of a young Jewish girl. God became man. Mary's baby son was called Jesus. He was like no one else. Jesus is both God and man.

Look It Up:
Isaiah 7:14

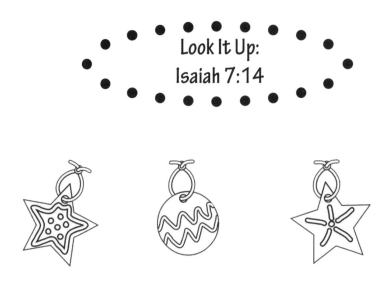

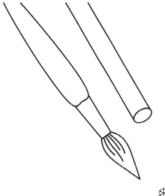

Bake Claydough Decorations

YOU WILL NEED:
✳200 g (7 oz) plain white flour ✳2 tbs salt
✳100 ml (3.3 fl oz) cold water
✳Large mixing bowl ✳Wooden spoon ✳Plastic bag

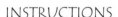

INSTRUCTIONS
Put the flour and salt in the large bowl.
Add the water, mixing thoroughly.
Knead into a soft ball.
Use straight away or keep in a plastic bag.

TO MAKE THE DECORATIONS
YOU WILL ALSO NEED:
A rolling pin, A baking tray , Biscuit cutters,
A drinking straw, Paints and pens,
Narrow ribbon or wool

1. Set your oven to a cool 110 degrees Celsius (Gas Mark 1/4; 225 degrees Fahrenheit).
2. Make the claydough. Roll it out to 5 mm (0.2 inches) thick.
3. Cut out some shapes with cutters.
4. Press out a hole in the top of each shape with the end of a drinking straw.
5. Place them on a baking tray and bake for 3 or 4 hours, until they are hard.
6. Decorate your shapes with felt tip pens, poster or acrylic paints. You could varnish the shapes when they are dry for a shiny, durable look.
7. Thread the ribbon or wool through the hole and hang them on the Christmas tree.

5. Zechariah's Promise

Look It Up:
Luke 1:5-25

Before the promised Saviour was born, another baby was born in Israel. This baby would grow up to be a man called John the Baptist. God would use John to remind people about the promised Saviour. John would actually show them who the promised Saviour was.

Before John was born, an angel appeared to his father, Zechariah, to tell him that his wife would give birth to this baby. Zechariah was a bit scared when he saw the angel, but the angel told him not to be afraid. 'You will have joy and gladness, and many will rejoice at his birth ... He will be filled with the Holy Spirit, even from his mother's womb. And he will turn many ... to the Lord their God.' Zechariah had doubts, however. The angel told him that, because he had not believed God's message, he would not be able to speak until the day his son was born. Zechariah should not have doubted. His wife, Elizabeth, soon realised that she was expecting a baby – even though she was quite old and had never had a baby before.

Zechariah Wordsearch

Can you find all the words hidden in the puzzle square?

ZECHARIAH

INCENSE

TEMPLE

HEROD

```
Z T Y X D O R E H
N E O B P Z L T J
P M C E A I E O M
R P Y H O B H W A
I L S T A N G E L
E E M Z B R P H E
S O I L D A I B Z
T L L E I R B A G
E S N E C N I J H
```

PRIEST

ANGEL

BABY

JOHN

ELIZABETH

GABRIEL

6. Mary's Promise

Many years after Isaiah's prophecy was made, an angel was sent to a young girl, called Mary, to tell her that she was the one chosen to be the mother of the promised Saviour.

The angel was called Gabriel. He was sent by God to the town of Nazareth. When he appeared to Mary he announced, 'Greetings, O favoured one, the Lord is with you!" Just as Zechariah had been a bit scared when he saw the angel, Mary was also troubled. But the angel told her not to be afraid. He explained to her that inside her womb there was a son and that she was to call him Jesus. 'He will be great, and will be called the Son of the Most High.' Mary asked the angel how this would happen. 'I'm not married and I've never known a man in that way,' she said. The angel told her, 'The Holy Spirit will come upon you, and the power of the Most High will overshadow you; therefore the child to be born will be called holy—the Son of God.'

The angel then told her that her cousin Elizabeth was also expecting. Mary was amazed at all this bewildering news. 'Let it be to me according to your word,' she said, obediently.

Look It Up:
Luke 1:26-38

Make a Christmas Angel

1. Trace or copy this pattern onto light white card.

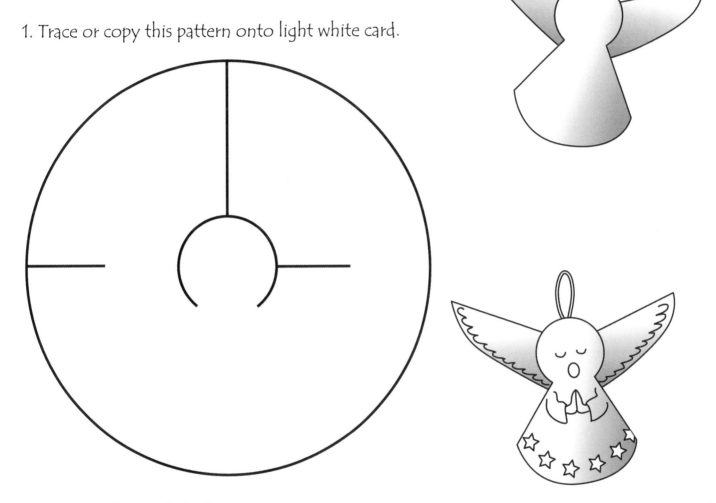

2. Cut out along all the lines.
3. The middle circle is the head. Bend your card round and slot the wings together along the short cuts. It might take a bit of practice! If you like, you can draw a face on the angel and decorate it before folding together.
4. Glue a loop onto the angel's head and hang it on the Christmas tree.

7. Mary and Elizabeth

Look It Up:
Luke 1:39-45

The next thing Mary did was to go into the hill country of Judah to visit her relative, Elizabeth. This is the same Elizabeth who was married to Zechariah and who was expecting her own baby son. Mary entered Elizabeth's house and called out a greeting. When Elizabeth heard Mary's voice, the baby inside her heard it too.

Babies can do that – they can hear what's going on outside in the world. Elizabeth's baby realised that the promised Saviour was nearby and he jumped inside his mother's womb. He was full of the Holy Spirit, just as the angel had promised. Elizabeth knew that Mary's unborn baby was the promised Saviour. She spoke out in a loud voice, 'Blessed are you among women, and blessed is the fruit of your womb! And why is this granted to me, that the mother of my Lord should come to me?'

MAZE

Mary hurried through the Judean hills to get to Elizabeth.
Help her find her way there safely!

8. Mary's Song

Mary was filled with the Holy Spirit too. She broke into song! She sang praises to God because he had sent a Saviour at last. God showed her that great things would happen. He had kept his promise that he had made to Abraham. God was showing mercy to sinners by saving them from the punishment they deserved … and it was her baby whom God had sent to do this.

When Mary arrived at Elizabeth's home, she was given a special song to sing by God. She sang about how wonderful God is, the amazing things he had done in the past and would do again in the future. Mary stayed with her relatives in Judah for three months and then returned home.

The following words need to be placed into the gaps in Mary's song. Read the Bible passage first, then with the Bible closed see if you can remember which word goes where.

Magnifies, Blessed, Strength, Proud, Exalted, Remembrance, God, Mighty, Good, Offspring, Humble, Holy, Thrones, Empty, Fear

Look It Up:
Luke 1:46-55

Missing Words

My soul _____ the Lord,
and my spirit rejoices in ___ my
Saviour, for he has looked on the
_____ estate of his servant.
For behold, from now on all
generations will call me _____;
for he who is _____has done great
things for me, and ____ is his name.
And his mercy is for those who ____
him from generation to generation.
He has shown _____ with his
arm; he has scattered the _____ in
the thoughts of their hearts; he has
brought down the mighty from their
_____ and _____ those of humble
estate; he has filled the hungry with
____ things, and the rich he has sent
away _____.
He has helped his servant Israel, in
_____ of his mercy,
as he spoke to our fathers, to Abraham
and to his _____ forever.

9. Joseph's Dream

There was a problem. Although Mary wasn't married, she was engaged to a man called Joseph. When the news came out that Mary was expecting a baby, Joseph was very upset. He didn't realise that the child inside her was the Son of God.

Joseph thought the best thing to do would be to put an end to the engagement quietly. But an angel appeared to him in a dream, saying, 'Joseph, son of David, do not fear to take Mary as your wife, for that which is conceived in her is from the Holy Spirit. She will bear a son, and you shall call his name Jesus, for he will save his people from their sins.' Joseph woke up and did as the angel of the Lord had commanded him. He married Mary, but did not love her in the way a husband does until she had given birth to her firstborn son. Joseph then named him Jesus.

Look It Up:
Matthew 1:18-25

Love Hearts

These hearts should remind us that Joseph loved his wife, Mary, but also that God is love. That's why he sent Jesus!

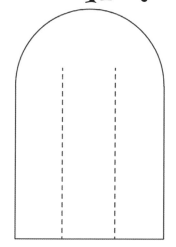

◄ Trace and cut out this template onto a piece of card.

Fold 2 pieces of different coloured paper in half and place the card template next to the fold on each one as shown. Cut out. Cut along the dotted lines too.

►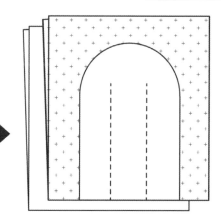

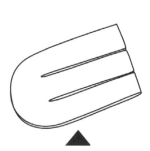

You now have 2 pieces like this. Look at the diagram.

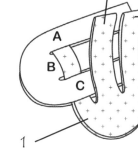

▲ Pay close attention to the parts that are labelled 1, 2 and 3 – and the other parts that are labelled a, b and c. The weaving should go as follows.

1. Arm 1 goes through arm C, then arm B goes through arm 1 and then arm 1 goes through arm A.

2. Arm 2 goes over arm C, then through arm B and then arm A goes through arm 2. ►

3. Arm 3 goes through arm C then arm B goes through arm 3 and then arm 3 goes through arm A.

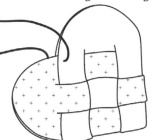

10. John's Birth

Look It Up:
Luke 1:57-66

When Elizabeth gave birth to a son, all her friends and relatives rejoiced. All young Jewish boys had to have a special ceremony to welcome them as people of God. It was at this time that a name was chosen. Elizabeth told her family that the baby was to be called John. Everyone was surprised. 'None of your relatives are called by this name,' they said. The friends and family decided to ask Zechariah what he thought. Zechariah asked them for a writing tablet. On it he wrote, 'His name is John.' And immediately Zechariah was able to speak. The first words he said, after such a long time of silence, were words about how great God was! Soon the news spread and everyone, across the country of Judea, was talking about what had happened. Everyone wondered just what sort of child John would be.

Colour in the picture. Can you spot Elizabeth, Zechariah and John? Unjumble the letters to find out what Zechariah wrote, then write it on the tablet in the picture.

isH amne si nohJ

Colour and Puzzle

11. Zechariah's Song

Just as Mary sang a song in praise of God, Zechariah did too. He sang about how great God was because he had sent a Saviour. God had remembered his holy promise, the promise he had given to Abraham. God had sent the Saviour to deliver those who believed in him from their greatest enemy – sin.

Then Zechariah sang about his son, John, 'You, child, will be called the prophet of the Most High; for you will go before the Lord to prepare his ways, to give knowledge of salvation to his people in the forgiveness of their sins, because of the tender mercy of our God.' Zechariah knew that his little boy would grow up to be the one who would tell people who God's Saviour was. And that Saviour was very nearly ready to be born.

Look It Up:
Luke 1:67-79

Crack the Code

Do you remember the code
we used to decipher Micah's message? Decode the first
part of Zechariah's song to the great God of Israel.

Luke 1:68

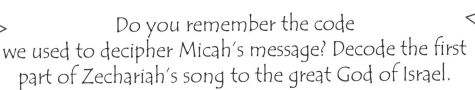

12. The Journey to Bethlehem

Look It Up:
Luke 2:4-7

Everyone in Israel had to return to their hometown so they could be counted. Joseph returned to Bethlehem. He took his wife, Mary, with him. When they arrived she gave birth to her firstborn son. She wrapped him in cloths and laid him in a manger because there was no room for them to stay in the inn. Micah's prophecy had come true!

1

2

3
Bridge over river – go to 9.

4

5

6
River floods – go back 2 spaces.

7

8

9

10
Lose the way – miss a turn.

11

12
Oasis! Go forward 2 spaces.

13

The Son of God was born in Bethlehem. God arranged everything perfectly so that this would happen. Look out for these stars in the game in order to get ahead. ✳✧❋

Fun and Games

✳ Read John 3:16 and move forward 1 space. ✧Read 1 John 4:9 and move forward 1 space. ❋ Read 1 John 4:16 and move forward 1 space.

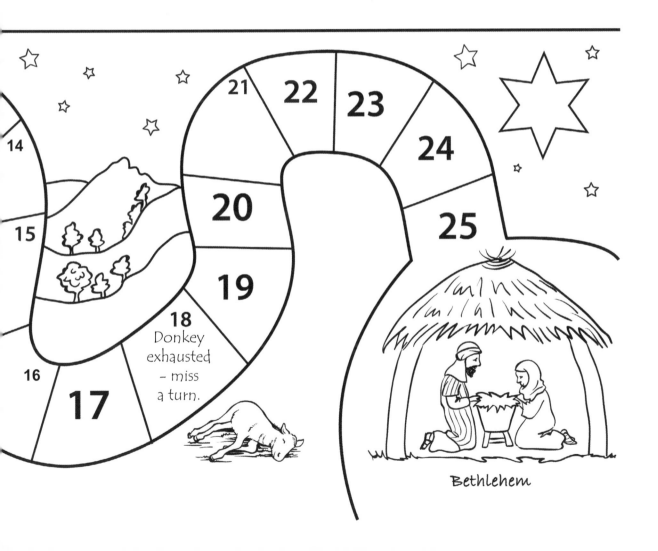

Bethlehem

13. The Shepherds Arrive

Look It Up:
Luke 2:8-20

Near Bethlehem, some shepherds kept watch over their flocks in the middle of the night. Suddenly an angel appeared to them. The glory of the Lord shone brightly around them and they were scared.

The angel told them not to be afraid. 'I bring you good news of great joy that will be for all the people. For unto you is born this day in the city of David a Saviour, who is Christ the Lord ... you will find a baby wrapped in swaddling cloths and lying in a manger.'

The whole sky was then filled with angels praising God and saying, 'Glory to God in the highest, and on earth peace among those with whom he is pleased!'

The shepherds rushed off to find the baby and then afterwards told everyone they met about the wonderful things they had seen and heard.

Make Some Christmas Cards

YOU WILL NEED:
Thin card in dark blue, white and yellow
Scissors and glue
Cotton wool or fleecy material
Markers
Stick-on stars

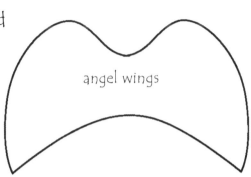

INSTRUCTIONS:
Fold a sheet of dark blue card in half to make a card. Cut out the angel body in white card and the wings in yellow card. Draw the face and arms onto the angel and stick it to the front of your folded blue card, near the top edge. Draw four legs and a face for the sheep in black marker below the angel, and glue on the cotton wool or fleece for the body. Decorate the 'sky' with stars!

You could also make the angels by themselves as a tree decoration.

14. Simeon's Saviour

Some time after Jesus' birth, he was taken to the temple in Jerusalem by his parents. There he was held in the arms of an old man called Simeon.

Simeon had been waiting for the arrival of God's Saviour for many years. And as soon as he saw the baby Jesus, he knew this was the one he had been waiting for.

Look It Up:
Luke 2:25-35

God had told him that he wouldn't die until he had seen the Saviour. Simeon took Jesus in his arms and blessed God and said, 'Lord, now you are letting your servant depart in peace, according to your word; for my eyes have seen your salvation.' He knew that the little boy he held his arms would be the one to save sinners from the punishment that their sin deserved. He was the Saviour!

Now it's wordsearch time. All the words you have to find in this puzzle are part of Simeon's story.

Simeon Wordsearch

J	H	P	E	S	O	J	Q	R	Y
P	E	A	C	E	E	I	W	U	N
T	U	R	V	S	N	P	M	O	B
E	G	I	U	Q	X	O	I	I	P
M	H	S	T	S	B	T	E	V	R
P	G	O	D	C	A	Z	C	A	A
L	H	F	W	V	B	L	O	S	Y
E	X	B	L	I	Y	N	E	B	E
M	L	A	O	K	Y	R	A	M	R
O	S	I	M	E	O	N	D	C	F

SIMEON	SALVATION
SAVIOUR	BABY
JESUS	PRAYER
GOD	JOSEPH
TEMPLE	MARY
JERUSALEM	PEACE

15. Horrid Herod

Look It Up:
Matthew 2:1-7

Jesus was still a young infant when wise men from the east arrived in Jerusalem asking, 'Where is he who has been born king of the Jews? For we saw his star when it rose and have come to worship him.'

When Herod, the King, heard of this, he was troubled. He gathered the chief religious leaders together and asked them about where God's promised Saviour was to be born. He knew about the prophecies, but he did not love or worship God. All he was concerned about was his own power. He didn't want someone else to take his place as king. The religious leaders told Herod about Micah's prophecy and about how God's Word said that the promised Saviour would be born in Bethlehem. Herod began to plot. He deceived the wise men into thinking that he wanted to worship the new king too. He told them to go and search carefully for the child and then come back and tell him, so that he could go and worship too.

Follow that Star!

The wise men followed the star to find the baby Jesus. Help them find their way to the King of kings!

16. The Wise Men Worship

Look It Up:
Matthew 2:9-12

The wise men left the city of Jerusalem and as they did so, they saw the star in the east once again. This star went before them, until it stopped over the place where the young child was.

The wise men were overjoyed when they realised they had arrived at their destination. They came up to the house where Jesus and his family were living and they fell down and worshipped the young child. They presented him with gifts of gold, frankincense and myrrh. These expensive and special gifts showed how much the wise men respected Jesus. He was just a baby, but he was also the Son of God. Jesus is the King of kings and Lord of lords. Once the wise men had worshipped the baby Jesus, they began their journey back home. Thankfully, an angel warned them about Herod's plot, so they left the country by a different route.

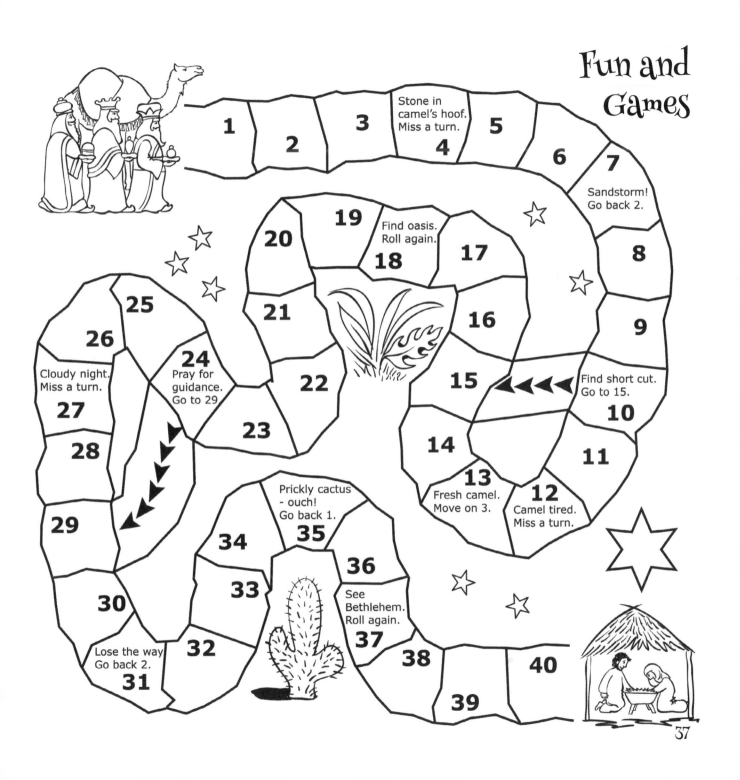

Fun and Games

1

2

3

Stone in camel's hoof. Miss a turn. 4

5

6

7 Sandstorm! Go back 2.

8

9

Find short cut. Go to 15. 10

11

12 Camel tired. Miss a turn.

13 Fresh camel. Move on 3.

14

15

16

17

18

Find oasis. Roll again.

19

20

21

22

23

24 Pray for guidance. Go to 29

25

26

Cloudy night. Miss a turn. 27

28

29

30

Lose the way Go back 2. 31

32

33

34

35 Prickly cactus - ouch! Go back 1.

36

See Bethlehem. Roll again. 37

38

39

40

37

17. The Escape to Egypt

Look It Up:
Matthew 2:13-23

After the wise men had left, an angel of the Lord appeared again to Joseph, in a dream, saying, 'Rise, take the child and his mother, and flee to Egypt and remain there until I tell you, for Herod is about to search for the child to destroy him.'

Then Joseph got up. He took Jesus and Mary, in the middle of the night, and left for the land of Egypt. They did this just in time. When Herod realised that the wise men had tricked him, he sent his soldiers to Bethlehem. The soldiers killed every young boy aged two and under. But Jesus was safe with his family in Egypt. They stayed there until they heard the news that Herod was dead.

Again, this escape to Egypt had been prophesied many years before, when the prophet Hosea passed on God's message, 'Out of Egypt I called my Son,' (Hosea 11:1).

Joseph heard that Herod's son was reigning instead of his father. An angel told him to take his young family back to Nazareth. Again this was just like a prophecy that had been given many years before, that God's promised Saviour would be called a Nazarene (Isaiah 11:1). Everything was beginning to fit together. It was all happening just as God had planned it would.

Handprint Angels!

God spoke to Joseph through his angel messengers. To make some handprint angel pictures, you will need: A big piece of paper, some poster or acrylic paint, a shallow palette or plate (one for each different colour that you use) and your hands!

Put some yellow paint on the plate, and squish your hands in it so they are covered with colour. Then get your paper and print two handprints next to each other - just like picture 1.

Then wash your hands and put some blue paint in another plate and make a handprint in the middle of the other two. Use two thumb prints to make 'arms' as shown in picture 2. Use your index finger to make a circle for the head. Swish your finger around on the paper if you need to make the head bigger. Make some red fingerprints round the head for 'hair'. You can paint in a face, halo and some stars around the angel with a brush or your fingers.

1.

2.

39

18. Abraham is Related to Jesus

Do you ever sit down with your relatives and listen to stories of years gone by? Grandparents can tell you about what it was like long ago in the days before television! They can tell you about relatives that died years and maybe even decades, before your parents were even born. Old people in your family were maybe told stories about their family by their grandparents. Just talking with your grandparents about the past could be very interesting!

Look It Up: Genesis 12:1-3

All these family members are what we call a family tree. Jesus had a family tree too. We know that Abraham was part of it. God had promised that Abraham would be a blessing to the whole world – and he was because Jesus was one of his descendants. Jesus blesses the whole world because he came to this world to save people from sin, no matter where they come from or what skin colour they have. The Bible tells us that people from every tribe and nation and language will worship God's Son.

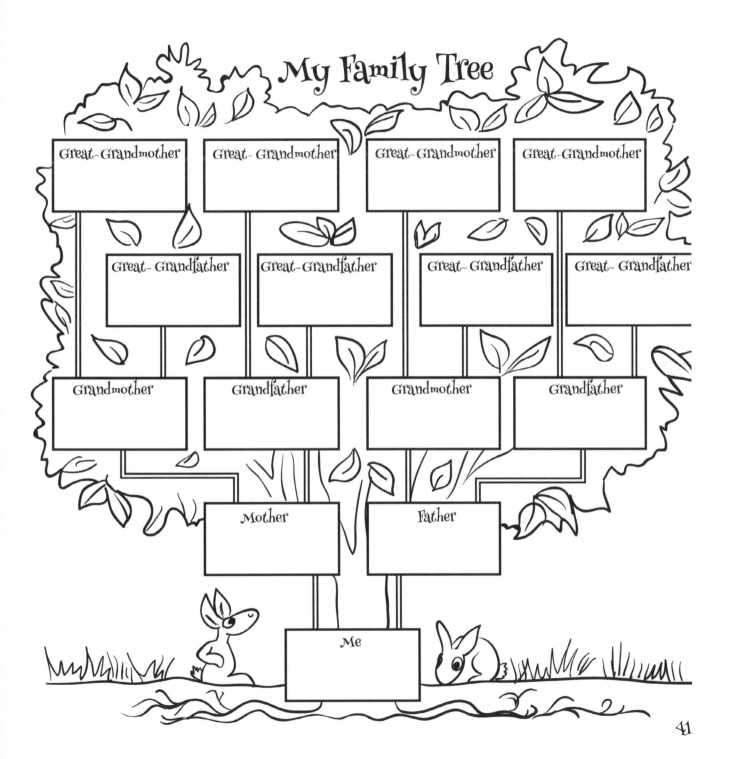

My Family Tree

Great-Grandmother

Great-Grandmother

Great-Grandmother

Great-Grandmother

Great-Grandfather

Great-Grandfather

Great-Grandfather

Great-Grandfather

Grandmother

Grandfather

Grandmother

Grandfather

Mother

Father

Me

19. David is Related to Jesus

Look It Up:
Matthew 1:1-17

David was the King of Israel, a great warrior and ruler. He wasn't perfect. He sinned against God by stealing another man's wife. But God showed mercy to David and both David and his son, Solomon, are in the family tree of Jesus.

Many of the messages that God gave to the prophets were about the fact that the promised Saviour would be from the family line of David. In the family tree of Jesus, (Matthew chapter 1) we can see that David is a direct ancestor of the Lord Jesus Christ.

Even some of the Psalms that David wrote are about this wonderful Saviour. In Psalm 22:1 we read the exact words that Jesus spoke when he died on the cross, 'My God, my God, why have you forsaken me?'

Make a Shiny Star

Did you know that the town of Bethlehem was also called the City of David? Bethlehem was where the wise men travelled to by following God's special star. Let's make some stars to remind us to follow God by obeying him.

When you have finished, you can write the following words in the centre of the stars: Believe, Trust, Love God, Love Others, Pray, Repent, Obey. Look up the following Bible verses to find out where God tells us to do these things:

* John 6:47 * Proverbs 3:5-6 * Matthew 22:37
* John 13:34 * Romans 12:12 * Matthew 3:2
* Acts 5:29

The star is easy to draw as it uses two triangles to make the six-pointed shape. Draw your own or use the template on this page. For each decoration, cut out one big star shape and two smaller ones from thin card in any colours you like. Punch a hole in a point of the big star. Take some small foam sticky pads and stick them on three points of a smaller star as shown in the picture. Peel off the paper and stick your small star in the centre of the larger one. Do the same on the other side. You now have a 3D star. Add a loop and hang on the tree or anywhere in your home.

20. Jesus is the Reason

Look It Up:
Matthew 14:13-21

Why do we celebrate Christmas? We do it because Jesus was born. God's plan was for his Son to become a human and live perfectly amongst people on earth.

This is what happened. Jesus lived a perfect life because nobody else could. The punishment for sin was placed on Jesus. Those who trusted in Jesus Christ would then be freed from the punishment of sin.

Jesus lived a life just like you and me – except he never sinned. He ate and drank and played – but didn't sin. He laughed and cried and slept – but didn't sin. He grew up just like a normal kid – but didn't sin. His life was the same as ours because he is human, but it was different to ours because he is totally without any sin because he is also God.

Because he is God he has great power. We can see his great power in all the miracles he did while he was on earth. He fed 5,000 people with just five loaves and two fish. He cured a blind man so that he could see again. He brought a young girl back to life. He calmed the sea, just by telling it to be quiet.

A Puzzle For You

Fill in the blanks.

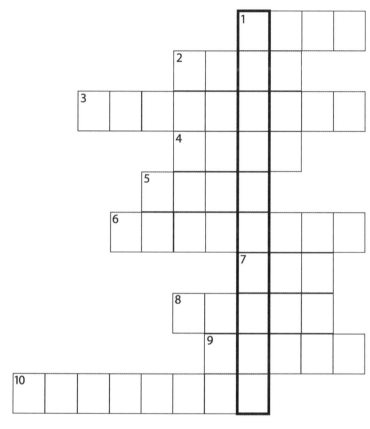

1. God's _____ was for God the Son to be born in Bethlehem

2. Jesus came to set sinners ____

3. Jesus was _____ from us because he didn't sin

4. As a child, Jesus had a normal ____

5. Jesus was the _____ as us because he was completely human.

6. The name for the amazing things that Jesus did.

7. How many fish did Jesus use to feed the 5,000 people?

8. Jesus healed a _____ man so he could see again.

9. Jesus showed his _____ over death when he brought a girl back to life.

10. Jesus calmed a storm and showed he is Lord of all _____.

Now read the letters in the middle downwards to find a word that describes what Jesus is.

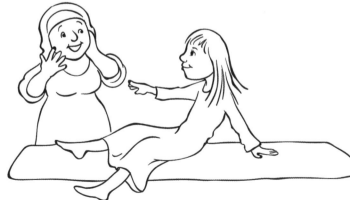

45

21. Jesus' Death

Look It Up:
Mark 15:1-39

The story of Jesus doesn't stop at Christmas. He grew up to be a man. It was when he was a man that he was arrested. The religious leaders were jealous of him, so they told the Romans to crucify Jesus. This was a horrible and cruel way to die. Jesus was nailed to a cross of wood. How horrible – but it was actually all part of God's plan.

Sin has to be punished, so someone had to die. This person had to be perfect, without sin. The only way that could happen was for God's Son to come to earth as a human being, live a perfect life and then be punished instead of sinners. This is what Jesus did.

When Jesus died, the whole world went dark. This shows us what a terrible thing it was for the Son of God to be treated like this. But a wonderful thing happened too – the thick curtain in the temple was torn from top to bottom. God did this. The curtain had kept people out of God's special holy place in the temple. But now, because Jesus had taken the punishment, sinners didn't have to be separated from God anymore.

If we trust in Jesus, we can come straight to God and be close to him – the best friend that anyone can have, the perfect Father. This is what Jesus' death has given us – peace with God.

Cross-words...

Jesus was crucified on a wooden cross. Here is a wordsearch in the shape of a cross. See if you can find the following words inside the puzzle. The words go up and down, right to left and diagonally.

GOD

CROSS

JESUS

DARK

TEMPLE

CURTAIN

ROMANS

JEWS

PEACE

ARRESTED

SAVIOUR

CHRIST

TORN

CRUCIFIXION

```
                        T  S  I  R  H  C
                        A  Q  J  P  E  O
                        R  B  D  E  M  F
                        H  J  C  G  S  N
                        C  T  L  S  K  U
          A  F  E  N  I  R  S  O  T  D  U  S  V  A  Q  L
          S  A  V  I  O  U  R  Z  R  Y  C  X  B  D  K  M
          G  B  J  D  K  C  O  P  X  N  W  P  E  A  C  E
          C  U  R  T  A  I  N  W  F  E  I  H  P  R  N  R
          H  I  C  M  L  F  R  Q  U  G  S  J  O  K  S  T
                        I  V  S  D  Y  W
                        X  T  W  E  U  E
                        I  V  Z  T  O  J
                        O  G  Y  S  V  X
                        N  O  X  E  W  Z
                        Y  D  N  R  F  S
                        L  M  K  R  N  E
                        D  C  Z  A  J  Q
                        T  E  M  P  L  E
                        P  O  T  B  G  I
                        R  S  A  H  U  R
```

47

22. Jesus is Alive!

Look It Up:
Mark 16:1-11

The story of Jesus doesn't end there, either. His body was taken down from the cross and put in a tomb.

Three days later, his friends came to the tomb to anoint his body with special spices. Angels were there and soon the news was out – Jesus had risen from the dead. One of Jesus' friends, Mary Magdalene, was upset when she discovered that Jesus' body wasn't in the tomb. Confused and crying, she asked someone, whom she thought was the gardener, where they had taken Jesus' body. When Jesus spoke to her, she recognised his voice immediately. Over the next few weeks, many people saw Jesus alive. The disciples, his special friends, even had a barbecue on the beach with Jesus.

Spiced Cookies

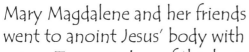

Mary Magdalene and her friends went to anoint Jesus' body with spices. To remind us of this loving act, we can make spiced Christmas cookies.

INGREDIENTS
100 g (3.5 oz) brown sugar
150 g (5.3 oz) golden syrup
1 teaspoon cinnamon
1 teaspoon ground ginger
1 teaspoon ground cloves
150 g (5.3 oz) butter
1 egg
1 teaspoon bicarbonate of soda
1 teaspoon cold water
450 g (15.9 oz) plain flour (if you want to make this gluten free use rice flour)
Icing and decorations

Put the sugar, syrup, butter and spices into a large saucepan and stir gently over low heat until the butter is melted. Take off the heat.
Dissolve the bicarbonate of soda in the water in a small cup.
Add the egg to the saucepan and stir. Then stir in the soda mixture. It will fizz and bubble!
Add the flour gradually, mixing well with a wooden spoon.
Put the dough in the fridge to cool for about 20 minutes.
Set oven to 170 degrees Celsius or Gas Mark 4 or 325 degrees Fahrenheit.
Roll out the dough on a lightly-floured surface to about 5 mm (0.2 inches) thick. Cut out shapes with cutters or a knife. Place on a baking tray and bake for about 8-10 minutes.
Decorate with icing, sprinkles, silver balls, raisins and small sweets.

23. The Greatest Gift

Look It Up:
John 3:16

As you get excited about all the gifts you will receive, remember that the greatest gift you could ever receive is Jesus himself. As you finish off wrapping the presents, that you are giving to others, remember that there are gifts you can give to God.

How is Jesus God's gift to you? If you were to live your life without trusting in Jesus, you would perish because sin has to be punished by God. But if you believe that because Jesus died on the cross your sins can be forgiven, then you are given the gift of forgiveness and the gift of everlasting life. All those who trust in Jesus will go to be with him in heaven, forever, when they die. Their body will die, but their soul will live for eternity. Your soul, the bit of you that loves God, will go to be with God, forever, in heaven.

Make Little Gift Boxes

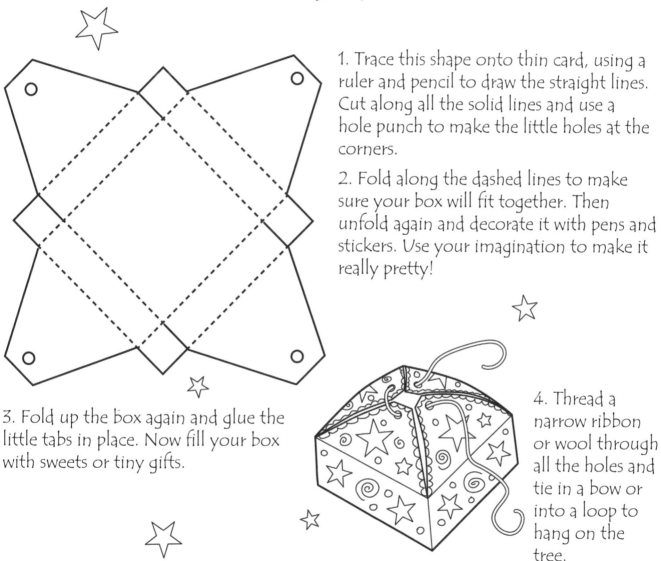

1. Trace this shape onto thin card, using a ruler and pencil to draw the straight lines. Cut along all the solid lines and use a hole punch to make the little holes at the corners.

2. Fold along the dashed lines to make sure your box will fit together. Then unfold again and decorate it with pens and stickers. Use your imagination to make it really pretty!

3. Fold up the box again and glue the little tabs in place. Now fill your box with sweets or tiny gifts.

4. Thread a narrow ribbon or wool through all the holes and tie in a bow or into a loop to hang on the tree.

If you want to make a box that is a bit bigger, there is another template on page 63 that you can use.

24. Your Gifts

Look It Up:
James 1:17

So what gifts can you give God? You can give him your trust. You can believe in him. You can repent and be truly sorry for the wrong things you have done. God wants to give you good gifts like forgiveness. In James 1:17 the Bible tells us that every good gift comes from God. He wants people to turn away from their sin and to trust and love him. There are lots of things that God can give us and we can give him. He gives us love, faith, eternal life and forgiveness. We can show God we love him by living a life that pleases him. In the wordsearch there are words to find, and they are all things that please God - gifts that we can give him.

Draw yourself praying to God. Write down what you will pray to God about.

God's Gifts Wordsearch

Find the gift words in the wordsearch.

```
S P A T I E N C E S
S X Z L M L O V E S
E P G Q O N J C K E
N I O U F P N I Q N
D Y O J A E Q R H E
N O D B I P G W S L
I S N D T R U S T T
K B E C H F T U V N
J B S D O N E M L E
O K S B E L I E F G
```

FAITH

LOVE

GENTLENESS

OBEDIENCE

TRUST

JOY

KINDNESS

BELIEF

GOODNESS

PATIENCE

25. Celebrate!

Look It Up:
1 Corinthians 6:14

And finally the big day arrives – Christmas Day. This is a day that lots of people celebrate because of the fact that Jesus was born. Remembering the fact that Jesus has a birthday is a good thing because it reminds us that Jesus is a human being. But we must also remember that he is God.

Jesus is God. He is all powerful and one day he is coming back. He will come back to this world, not as a helpless baby – but as a powerful victor. Everything will be made new. There will be new heavens and a new earth (2 Peter 3:13). The bodies of those who trusted in Jesus in the past will be reunited with their spirits. These bodies will be perfect with no hurts or diseases. God's people will no longer sin and they will live with God.

Jesus is alive and is in heaven right now. If you trust in Jesus and ask God to forgive your sins, you can be certain that one day you will be there with him. It will be a greater and far more exciting day than the 25th of December.

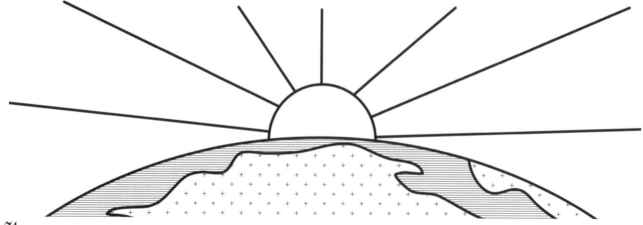

Crown Him!

Jesus, the baby born at Christmas, is coming back. He will be King over all. Let's make crowns to remind ourselves of this wonderful fact.

Get a piece of paper or card about 12 x 65 cm (4.72 x 25.6 inches) (you might need two pieces together). You will need scissors, glue, pens, stickers, paint and anything else you would like to decorate your crown with.

First, draw and cut out the shape of your crown (here are some ideas).

| simple | more tricky! | cross |

Make sure it fits around your head, but don't glue it yet. Get busy with the pens, paint, stickers and decorations. You might like to stick on pieces of fabric, ribbons, or fake jewels. Make it really sparkling and regal! When it is dry, you can curve it round and stick with glue or sellotape.

Wear your crown with pride at Christmas dinner!

25 Bible Readings

1. Genesis 3:14-15

2. Genesis 12:2-3

3. Micah 5:2

4. Isaiah 7:14

5. Luke 1:5-25

6. Luke 1:26-38

7. Luke 1:39-45

8. Luke 1:46-55

9. Matthew 1:18-25

10. Luke 1:57-66

11. Luke 1:67-79

12. Luke 2:4-7

13.　Luke 2:8-20

14.　Luke 2:25-35

15.　Matthew 2:1-7

16.　Matthew 2:9-12

17.　Matthew 2:13-23

18.　Genesis 12:1-3

19.　Matthew 1:1-17

20.　Matthew 14:13-21

21.　Mark 15:1-39

22.　Mark 16:1-11

23.　John 3:16

24.　James 1:17

25.　1 Corinthians 6:14

Well done for completing all these Bible readings!

Jesus' Death

Pilate said to them, "Then what shall I do with Jesus who is called Christ?" They all said,

"Let him be crucified!"
Matthew 27:22

Jesus' Resurrection

Do not be alarmed. You seek Jesus of Nazareth, who was crucified. He has risen; he is not here. See the place where they laid him.

Mark 16:6

Answers

Chapter 1: Angel (Yellow), Clothes (brown), Tree (brown/green), Sword (silver), Hair (black), Snake (red/yellow).

Chapter 3: Yet out of you shall come forth to me the one to be ruler in Israel.

Chapter 5: See page 61.

Chapter 8: My soul magnifies the Lord, and my spirit rejoices in God my Saviour, for he has looked on the humble estate of his servant. For behold, from now on all generations will call me blessed; for he who is mighty has done great things for me, and holy is his name. And his mercy is for those who fear him from generation to generation. He has shown strength with his arm; he has scattered the proud in the thoughts of their hearts; he has brought down the mighty from their thrones and exalted those of humble estate; he has filled the hungry with good things, and the rich he has sent away empty. He has helped his servant Israel, in remembrance of his mercy, as he spoke to our fathers, to Abraham and to his offspring for ever.

Chapter 10: His name is John.

Chapter 11: Blessed be the Lord God of Israel for he has visited and redeemed his people and has raised up a horn of salvation for us in the house of his servant David.

Chapter 14: See page 61.

Chapter 20: Plan, Free, Different, Life, Same, Miracles, Two, Blind, Power, Creation, Perfection.

Chapter 21 and Chapter 24: See page 62.

Activity 5/Wordsearch answer

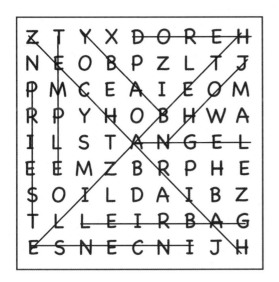

Activity 14/Wordsearch answer

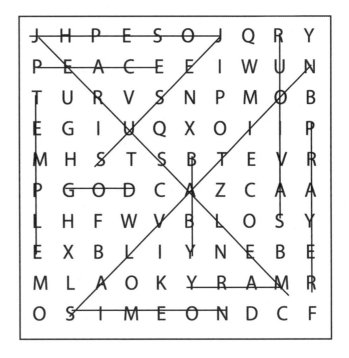

Activity 21/Wordsearch answer

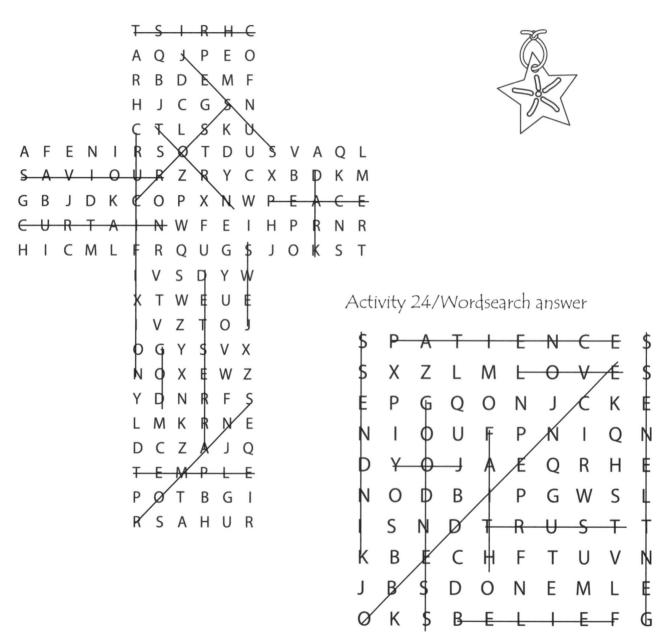

T S I R H C
A Q J P E O
R B D E M F
H J C G S N
C T L S K U
A F E N I R S O T D U S V A Q L
S A V I O U R Z R Y C X B D K M
G B J D K C O P X N W P E A C E
C U R T A I N W F E I H P R N R
H I C M L F R Q U G S J O K S T
I V S D Y W
X T W E U E
V Z T O J
O G Y S V X
N O X E W Z
Y D N R F S
L M K R N E
D C Z A J Q
T E M P L E
P O T B G I
R S A H U R

Activity 24/Wordsearch answer

S P A T I E N C E S
S X Z L M L O V E S
E P G Q O N J C K E
N I O U F P N I Q N
D Y O J A E Q R H E
N O D B P G W S L
I S N D T R U S T T
K B E C H F T U V N
J B S D O N E M L E
O K S B E L I E F G

62

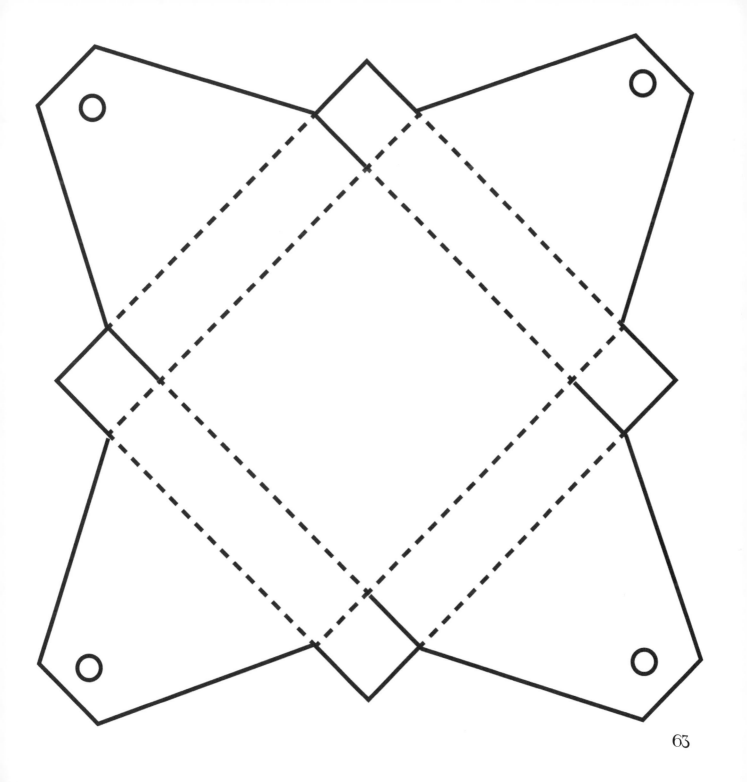

Christian Focus Publications

Christian Focus Publications publishes books for adults and children under its four main imprints: Christian Focus, CF4K, Mentor and Christian Heritage. Our books reflect our conviction that God's Word is reliable and Jesus is the way to know him, and live for ever with him. Our children's list includes a Sunday School curriculum that covers pre-school to early teens, and puzzle and activity books. We also publish personal and family devotional titles, biographies and inspirational stories that children will love. If you are looking for quality Bible teaching for children, then we have an excellent range of Bible stories and age-specific theological books. From pre-school board books to teenage apologetics, we have it covered!

CF4•K
Because you're never
too young to know Jesus

CHRISTIAN FOCUS PUBLICATIONS

Christian Focus | Christian Heritage | CF4K | Mentor

My
Christmas Activity
Calendar

Tick off each picture when you've
done each day's activity

1

2

3

4

21

22

23

24

Jesus is the Reason for the Season

25